ABC's
for
Girls

by Michael Kracht

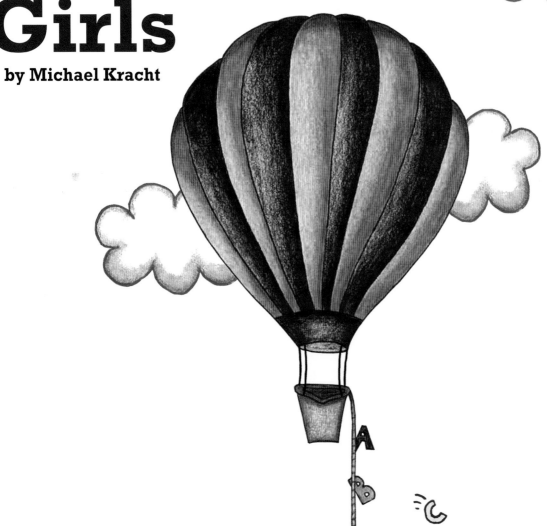

Majella Publishing

_____

ABC's for Girls
Copyright © 2017 by Michael Kracht

First published in the United States of America in 2017 by
Majella Publishing LLC

First Edition

10 9 8 7 6 5 4 3 2 1

Library of Congress Control Number: 2017900291

ISBN: 978-0-692-83173-1

Manufactured in China

All illustrations for this book were hand drawn in color pencil
by Michael Kracht through inspiration from his
children in heaven.

Hand drawn for my kids in heaven.

A

Apple pie

B

Butterfly

C

Castle

D

Dog

E

Elephant

F

Flower

G

Goldfish

H

Horse

I

Ice cream

J

Jewelry box

K

Kite

L

Ladybug

M

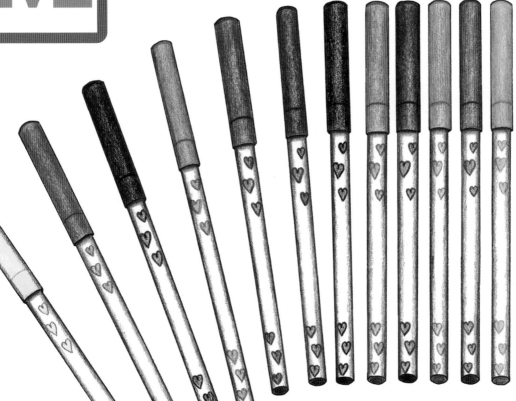

Markers

Numbers

O

Owl

P

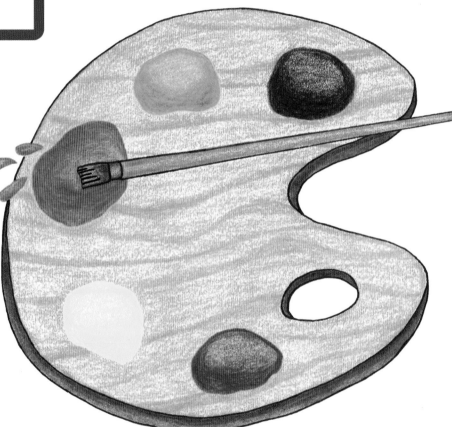

ABC

Paint

Q

Quilt

R

Rainbow

S

Seashell

T

Tea set

U

Umbrella

V

Violin

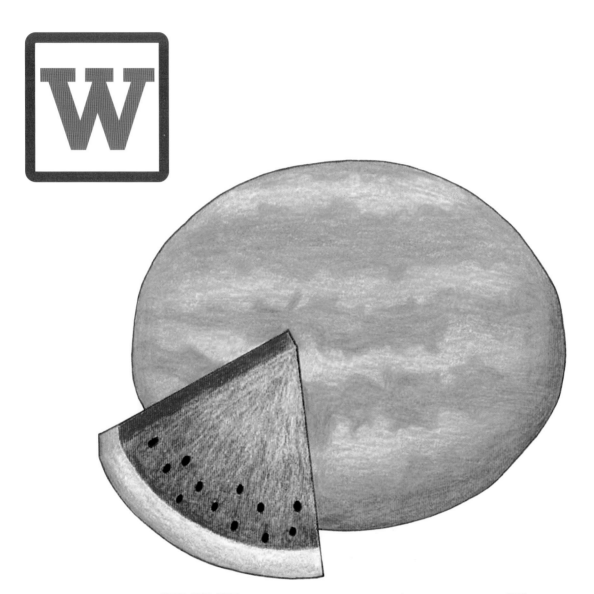

Watermelon

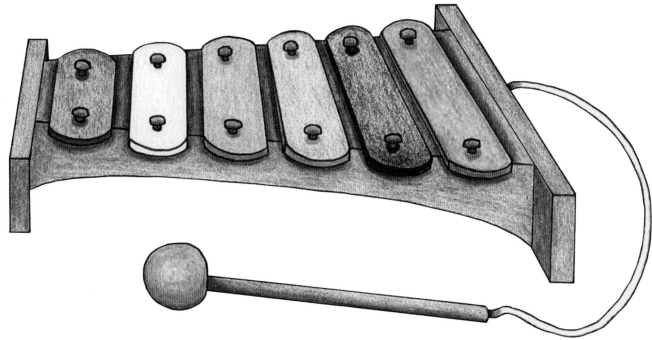

Xylophone

Y

Yo-yo

Z

Zoo